THE FIR TREE

Hans Christian Andersen's

THE FIR TREE

Illustrated by Nancy Ekholm Burkert

Harper & Row, Publishers

New York, Evanston, and London

This translation of THE FIR TREE by H. W. Dulcken.
Grateful acknowledgment is made for permission
to reprint a portion of Hymn VI,
"The Presentation of Christ in the Temple,"
from Poems *by Christopher Smart,*
edited with an Introduction and Notes by Robert Brittain.

THE FIR TREE by Hans Christian Andersen
 Printed in the United States of America. For information address Harper & Row, Publishers, Inc., 49 East 33rd Street, New York, N.Y. 10016. Published simultaneously in Canada by Fitzhenry & Whiteside Limited, Toronto. Library of Congress Catalog Card Number: 73-121800

THE FIR TREE

To Bob

"I speak for all—for them that fly,

And for the race that swim;

For all that dwell in moist and dry,

Beasts, reptiles, flow'rs and gems to vie

When gratitude begins her hymn."

Christopher Smart

1722–1771

OUT IN THE FOREST stood a pretty little Fir Tree. It had a good place; it could have sunlight, air there was in plenty, and all around grew many larger comrades—pines as well as firs. But the little Fir Tree wished ardently to become greater. It did not care for the warm sun and the fresh air; it took no notice of the peasant children, who went about talking together when they had come out to look for strawberries and raspberries.

Often they came with a whole potful, or had strung berries on a straw. Then they would sit down by the little Fir Tree and say, "How pretty and small that one is!" and the Tree did not like to hear that at all.

"Oh, if I were only as great a tree as the others!" sighed the little Fir. "Then I would spread my branches far around, and look out from my crown into the wide world. The birds would then build nests in my boughs, and when the wind blew, I could nod just as grandly as the others yonder."

He took no pleasure in the sunshine, in the birds, and in the red clouds that went sailing over him morning and evening. When it was winter and the snow lay all around, white and sparkling, a hare would often come jumping along, and spring right over the little Fir. Oh! this made him so angry.

But two winters went by, and when the third came, the little Tree had grown so tall that the hare was obliged to run around it.

"Oh! to grow, to grow, and become old; that's the only fine thing in the world," thought the Tree.

In the autumn, woodcutters always came and felled a few of the largest trees; that was done this year too. And the little Fir Tree, which was now quite well grown, shuddered with fear, for the great stately trees fell to the ground with a crash, and their branches were cut off, so that the trees looked quite naked, long, and slender—they could hardly be recognized. But then they were laid upon wagons, and horses dragged them away out of the wood. Where were they going? What destiny awaited them?

In the spring, when the Swallows and the Stork came, the Tree asked them, "Do you know where they were taken? Did you not meet them?"

The Swallows knew nothing about it, but the Stork looked thoughtful, nodded his head, and said, "Yes, I think so. I met many new ships when I flew out of Egypt; on the ships were stately masts. I fancy that these were the trees. They smelt like fir. I can assure you they're stately—very stately."

"Oh, that I were only big enough to go over the sea! What kind of thing is this sea, and how does it look?"

"It would take too long to explain all that," said the Stork, and he went away.

"Rejoice in thy youth," said the Sunbeams. "Rejoice in thy fresh growth, and in the young life that is within thee."

And the wind kissed the Tree, and the dew wept tears upon it; but the Fir Tree did not understand that.

When Christmas time approached, quite young trees were felled, sometimes trees which were neither so old nor so large as this Fir Tree that never rested but always wanted to go away. These young trees, which were almost the most beautiful, kept all their branches; they were put upon wagons, and horses dragged them away out of the wood.

"Where are they all going?" asked the Fir Tree. "They are not greater than I—indeed one of them was much smaller. Why do they keep all their branches? Whither are they taken?"

"We know that! We know that!" chirped the Sparrows. "Yonder in the town we looked in at the windows. We know where they go. Oh! they are dressed up in the greatest pomp and splendor that can be imagined. We have looked in at the windows, and have perceived that they are planted in the middle of the warm room, and adorned with the most beautiful things—gilt apples, honey cakes, playthings, and many hundreds of candles."

"And then?" asked the Fir Tree, and trembled

through all its branches. "And then? What happens then?"

"Why, we have not seen anything more," said the Sparrows. "But it was incomparable."

"Perhaps I may be destined to tread this glorious

path one day!" cried the Fir Tree rejoicingly. "That is even better than travelling across the sea. How painfully I long for it! If it were only Christmas now! Now I am great and grown-up, like the rest who were led away last year. Oh, if I were only on the carriage! If I were only in the warm room, among all the pomp and splendor! And then? Yes, then something even better will come, something far more charming, or else why should they adorn me so? There must be something grander, something greater still to come, but what? Oh! I'm suffering, I'm longing! I don't know, myself, what is the matter with me!"

"Rejoice in us," said Air and Sunshine. "Rejoice in thy fresh youth here in the woodland."

But the Fir Tree did not rejoice at all, but it grew

and grew. Winter and summer it stood there, green, dark green. The people who saw it said, "That's a handsome tree!" and at Christmas time it was felled before any one of the others. The axe cut deep into its marrow, and the tree fell to the ground with a sigh. It felt a pain, a sensation of faintness, and could not think at all of happiness, for it was sad at parting from its home, from the place where it had grown up. It knew that it should never again see the dear old companions, the little bushes and flowers all around—perhaps not even the birds. The parting was not at all agreeable.

The Tree only came to itself when it was unloaded in a yard, with the other trees, and heard a man say, "This one is perfect; we only want this one!"

Now two servants came, in gay liveries, and carried the Fir Tree into a large, beautiful saloon. All around the walls hung pictures, and by the great stove stood large Chinese vases with lions on the covers. There were rocking chairs, silken sofas, great tables covered with picture books, and toys worth a hundred times a hundred dollars—at least the children said so. And the Fir Tree was put into a great tub filled with sand; but no one could see that it was a tub, for it was hung round with green cloth, and stood on a large, many-colored carpet. Oh, how the Tree trembled! What was to happen now? The servants and the young ladies, also, decked it out. On one branch they hung little nets cut out of colored paper—every net was filled with sweetmeats; golden apples and walnuts hung down

as if they grew there; and more than a hundred little candles, red, white, and blue, were fastened to the different boughs. Dolls that looked exactly like real people—the Tree had never seen such before—swung upon the foliage, and high on the summit of the Tree was fixed a tinsel star. It was splendid, particularly splendid.

"This evening," said all, "this evening it will shine."

"Oh," thought the Tree, "that it were evening already! Oh, that the lights may be soon lit up! When may that be done? I wonder if trees will come out of the forest to look at me? Will the Sparrows fly against the panes? Shall I grow fast here, and stand adorned in summer and winter?"

Yes, he did not guess badly. But he had a complete backache from mere longing, and the backache is just as bad for a tree as the headache for a person.

At last the candles were lighted. What a brilliance, what splendor! The Tree trembled so in all its branches that one of the candles set fire to a green twig, and it was scorched.

"Heaven preserve us!" cried the young ladies, and they hastily put the fire out.

Now the Tree might not even tremble. Oh, that was terrible! It was so afraid of setting fire to some of its ornaments, and it was quite bewildered with all the brilliance. And now the folding doors were thrown open, and a number of children rushed in as if they would have overturned the whole Tree; the older people followed more deliberately. The little ones stood quite silent, but only for a minute; then they shouted till the room rang.

They danced gleefully round the Tree, and one present after another was plucked from it.

"What are they about?" thought the Tree. "What's going to be done?"

And the candles burned down to the twigs, and as they burned down they were extinguished, and then the children received permission to plunder the Tree. Oh! they rushed in upon it, so that every branch cracked again. If the Tree had not been fastened by the top and by the golden star to the ceiling, it would have fallen down.

The children danced about with their pretty toys. No one looked at the Tree except one old man, who came up and peeped among the branches, but only to see if a fig or an apple had not been forgotten.

"A story! A story!" shouted the children, and they drew a little fat man toward the Tree, and he sat down just beneath it—"for then we shall be in the green wood," said he, "and the tree may have the advantage of listening to my tale. But I can only tell one. Will you hear the story of Ivede-Avede, or of Klumpey-Dumpey, who fell downstairs, and still was raised up to honor and married the Princess?"

"Ivede-Avede!" cried some. "Klumpey-Dumpey!" cried others. And there was a great crying and shouting. Only the Fir Tree was quite silent, and thought, "Shall I not be in it? Shall I have nothing to do in it?" But he had been in the evening's amusement, and had done what was required of him.

And the fat man told about Klumpey-Dumpey, who fell downstairs, and yet was raised to honor and married the Princess. And the children clapped their hands, and cried, "Tell another! Tell another!" for they wanted to hear about Ivede-Avede. But they only got the story of Klumpey-Dumpey. The Fir Tree stood quite silent and thoughtful; never had the birds in the wood told such a story as that. Klumpey-Dumpey fell downstairs, and yet came to honor and married the Princess!

"Yes, so it happens in the world!" thought the Fir Tree, and believed it must be true, because that was such a nice man who had told it. "Well, who can know? Perhaps I shall fall downstairs too, and marry a Princess!" And it looked forward with pleasure to being adorned again, the next evening, with candles and toys, gold and fruit. "Tomorrow I shall not tremble," it thought. "I will rejoice in all my splendor. Tomorrow I shall hear the story of Klumpey-Dumpey again and, perhaps, that of Ivede-Avede too." And the Tree stood all night, quiet and thoughtful.

In the morning the servants and the chambermaid came in.

"Now my splendor will begin afresh," thought the Tree. But they dragged him out of the room, and upstairs to the garret, and here they put him in a dark corner where no daylight shone.

"What's the meaning of this?" thought the Tree. "What am I to do here? What is to happen?"

And he leaned against the wall, and thought and thought. And he had time enough, for days and nights went by and nobody came up; and when at length someone came, it was only to put some great boxes in a corner. Now the Tree stood quite hidden away, and the supposition was that it was quite forgotten.

"Now it's winter outside," thought the Tree.

"The earth is hard and covered with snow, and people cannot plant me. Therefore I suppose I'm to be sheltered here until spring comes. How considerate that is! How good people are! If it were only not so dark here, and so terribly solitary—not even a little hare! That was pretty out there in the wood, when the snow lay thick and the hare sprang past; yes, even when he jumped over me—but then I did not like it. It is terribly lonely up here!"

"Piep! Piep!" said a little Mouse, and crept forward. And then came another little one. They smelt at the Fir Tree, and then slipped among the branches.

"It's horribly cold," said the two little Mice, "or else it would be comfortable here. Don't you think so, you old Fir Tree?"

"I'm not old at all," said the Fir Tree. "There are many much older than I."

"Where do you come from?" asked the Mice. "And what do you know?" They were dreadfully inquisitive. "Tell us about the most beautiful spot on earth. Have you been there? Have you been in the storeroom, where the cheeses lie on the shelves and hams hang from the ceiling, where one dances on tallow candles, and goes in thin and comes out fat?"

"I don't know that!" replied the Tree. "But I know the wood, where the sun shines and where the birds sing."

And then it told all about its youth. The little Mice had never heard anything of the kind;

and they listened and said, "What a number of things you have seen! How happy you must have been!"

"I?" said the Fir Tree, and it thought about what it had told. "Yes, those were really quite happy times." But then he told of the Christmas Eve, when he had been hung with sweetmeats and candles.

"Oh!" said the little Mice, "how happy you have been, you old Fir Tree!"

"I'm not old at all," said the Tree. "I only came out of the wood this winter. I'm only rather backward in my growth."

"What splendid stories you can tell!" said the little Mice.

And the next night they came with four other

little Mice, to hear what the Tree had to relate. And the more it said, the more clearly did it remember everything, and thought, "Those were quite merry days! But they may come again. Klumpey-Dumpey fell downstairs, and yet he married the Princess. Perhaps I may marry a Princess too!" And then the Fir Tree thought of a pretty little Birch Tree that grew out in the forest. For the Fir Tree, that Birch was a real Princess.

"Who's Klumpey-Dumpey?" asked the little Mice.

And then the Fir Tree told the whole story. It could remember every single word, and the little Mice were ready to leap to the very top of the tree with pleasure. Next night a great many more Mice came, and on Sunday even two Rats appeared. But these thought the story was not pretty, and the little Mice were sorry for that, for now they also did not like it so much as before.

"Do you only know one story?" asked the Rats.

"Only that one," replied the Tree. "I heard it on the happiest evening of my life; I did not think then how happy I was."

"It's a very miserable story. Don't you know any about bacon and tallow candles—a storeroom story?"

"No," said the Tree.

"Then we'd rather not hear you," said the Rats. And they went back to their own people. The little Mice at last stayed away also, and then the Tree sighed and said, "It was very nice when they sat around me, the merry little Mice, and listened when I spoke to them. Now that's past too. But I shall remember to be pleased when they take me out."

But when did that happen? Why, it was one morning that people came and rummaged in the garret. The boxes were put away, and the Tree brought out. They certainly threw him rather roughly on the floor, but a servant dragged him away at once to the stairs, where the daylight shone.

"Now life is beginning again!" thought the Tree.

It felt the fresh air and the first sunbeams, and now it was out in the courtyard. Everything passed so quickly that the Tree quite forgot to look at itself, there was so much to look at all round. The courtyard was close to a garden, and here everything was blooming. The roses hung fresh and fragrant over the little paling, the linden trees were in blossom, and the Swallows cried, "Quinze-wit! Quinze-wit! My husband's come!" But it was not the Fir Tree that they meant.

"Now I shall live!" said the Tree rejoicingly, and spread its branches far out. But, alas! they were all withered and yellow, and the Tree lay in the corner among nettles and weeds. The tinsel star was still upon it, and shone in the bright sunshine.

In the courtyard were playing a couple of the

merry children who had danced round the Tree at Christmas time, and had rejoiced over it. One of the youngest ran up and tore off the golden star.

"Look what is sticking to the ugly old fir tree," said the child, and he trod upon the branches till they cracked again under his boots.

And the Tree looked at all the blooming flowers and the splendor of the garden, and then looked at itself, and wished it had remained in the dark corner of the garret. It thought of its fresh youth in the wood, of the merry Christmas Eve, and of the little Mice which had listened so pleasantly to the story of Klumpey-Dumpey.

"Past! past!" said the old Tree. "Had I but rejoiced when I could have done so! Past! past!"

And the servant came and chopped the Tree into little pieces; a whole bundle lay there. It blazed brightly under the great brewing copper, and it sighed deeply, and each sigh was like a little shot. And the children who were at play there ran up and seated themselves at the fire, looked into it, and cried, "Puff! Puff!" But at each explosion,

which was a deep sigh, the tree thought of a summer day in the woods, or of a winter night there, when the stars beamed; he thought of Christmas Eve and of Klumpey-Dumpey, the only story he had ever heard or knew how to tell. And then the Tree was burned.

The boys played in the garden, and the youngest had on his breast a golden star, which the Tree had worn on its happiest evening. Now that was past, and the Tree's life was past, and the story is past too: Past! past!—and that's the way with all stories.

The full-color illustrations by Nancy Ekholm Burkert
were executed in brush and inks;
the black and white drawings in pencil.
Designed by Gloria Bressler and Nancy Ekholm Burkert
Set in Caslon #471
Composed by The Composing Room, Inc.
Color separation and lithography by Neff Lithographing Company, Inc.
Bound by A. Horowitz & Son
Harper & Row, Publishers, Inc.

70717273876543 2 1